Show Hour Time

Draw hands on the clock face to show the time.
Write the time on the digital clock.

5 o'clock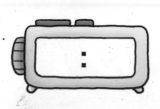

10 o'clock

6 o'clock

12 o'clock

3 o'clock

8 o'clock

Telling Time on the Hour

Minutes in an Hour

It takes the minute hand **5** minutes to move from one number to the next.

Count the minutes by **5**s.
Write the minutes on each line.

How many minutes in an hour? _____

How Many Minutes?

Look at the clock. Find the numbers 1 to 60 around the clock face.

Circle these numbers: **15 30 45 60**

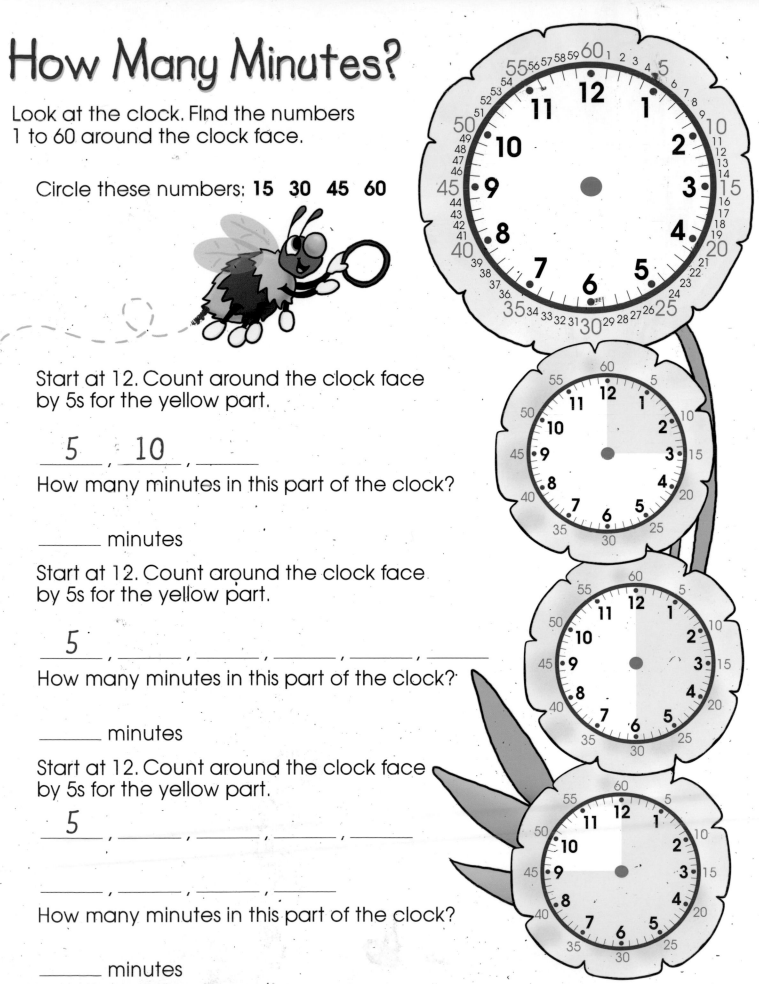

Start at 12. Count around the clock face by 5s for the yellow part.

__5__, __10__, _____

How many minutes in this part of the clock?

_____ minutes

Start at 12. Count around the clock face by 5s for the yellow part.

__5__, _____, _____, _____, _____, _____

How many minutes in this part of the clock?

_____ minutes

Start at 12. Count around the clock face by 5s for the yellow part.

__5__, _____, _____, _____,

_____, _____, _____, _____

How many minutes in this part of the clock?

_____ minutes

Counting Minutes in Half and Quarter Hours

Half Past the Hour

The long hand tells the minutes. When the minute hand points to **6**, we say **half past** the hour. The minute hand is *halfway* around the clock. The hour hand is *halfway* between the hour numbers.

The hour hand is halfway between **2** and **3**.
The minute hand points to **6**.

The time is **half past 2,** or **2:30**.

It is 30 minutes after 2.
It is **2:30**.

We can say: **"two thirty"**

Read the hour hand first. Then read the minute hand.
Write the time.

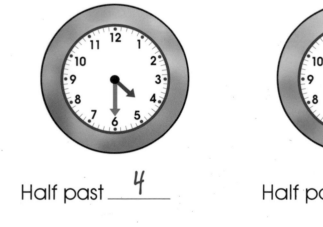

Half past ___4___

___4___ : ___30___

Half past _____

___ : ___

Half past _____

___ : ___

Half past _____

___ : ___

Half past _____

___ : ___

Half past _____

___ : ___

Telling Time on the Half Hour

Show Half Past

Draw hands on the clock or fill in the blanks to show the time.

Half past ___8___

"__eight__ thirty"

8 : 30

Half past _____

"_____ thirty"

3 : 30

Half past _____

"twelve _____"

___ : 30

Half past **5**

"_____ _____"

___ : ___

Earlier or Later

First, write the time or draw the hands in the **NOW** column.
Then, write the time for one hour earlier and one hour later.

One Hour Earlier **NOW** **One Hour Later**

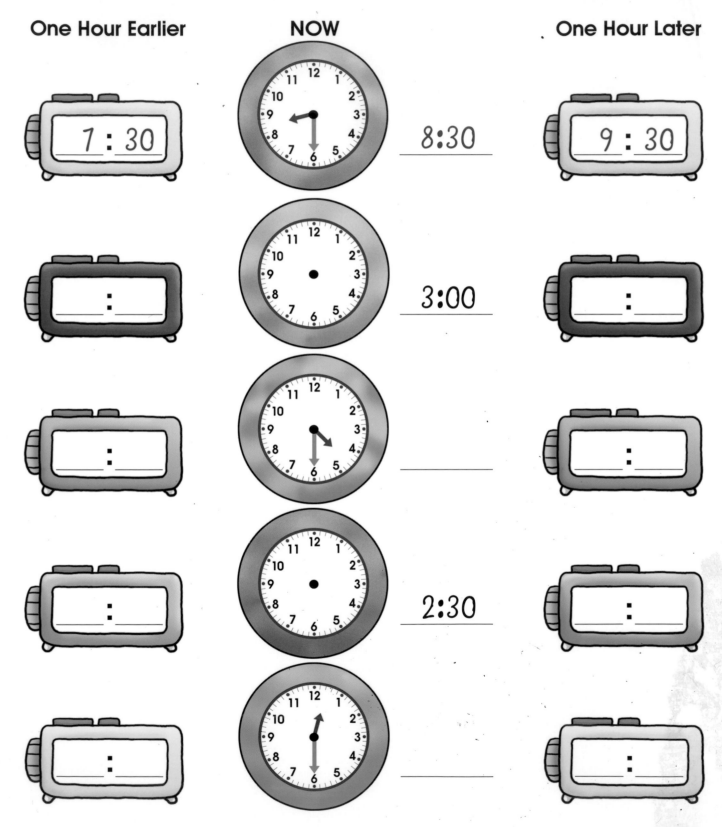

Row 1: 7 : 30 — (clock showing 8:30) 8:30 — 9 : 30

Row 2: _ : _ — (blank clock) 3:00 — _ : _

Row 3: _ : _ — (clock showing 6:20) _____ — _ : _

Row 4: _ : _ — (blank clock) 2:30 — _ : _

Row 5: _ : _ — (clock showing 12:00) _____ — _ : _

Finding Elapsed Time

Quarter Past the Hour

When the minute hand points to **3**, it is a quarter of the way around the clock. It is a **quarter past** the hour. The hour hand is a little past **2:00**.

The time is **quarter past 2**.

It is 15 minutes after 2.
It is **2:15**.

We can say: **"a quarter after 2"**

Read the hour hand first. Then read the minute hand.
Write the time.

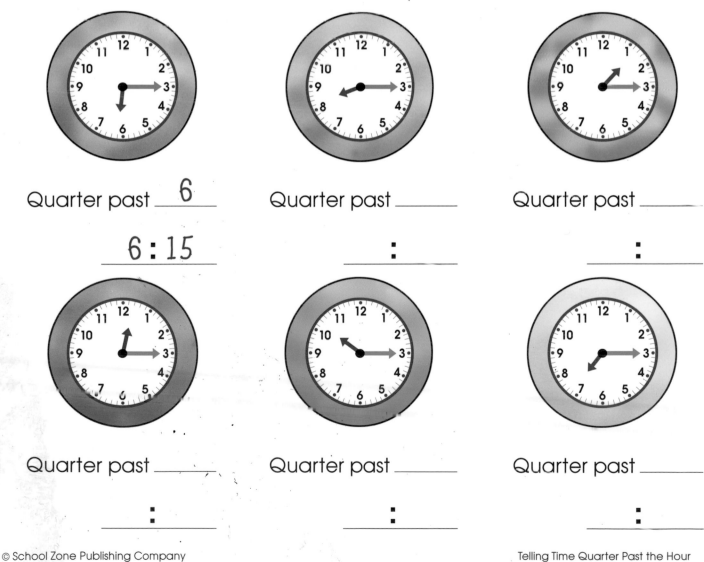

Quarter past ___6___

6 : 15

Quarter past _____

___ : ___

Quarter past _____

___ : ___

Quarter past _____

___ : ___

Quarter past _____

___ : ___

Quarter past _____

___ : ___

Show Quarter Past

Draw hands on the clock or fill in the blanks to show the time.

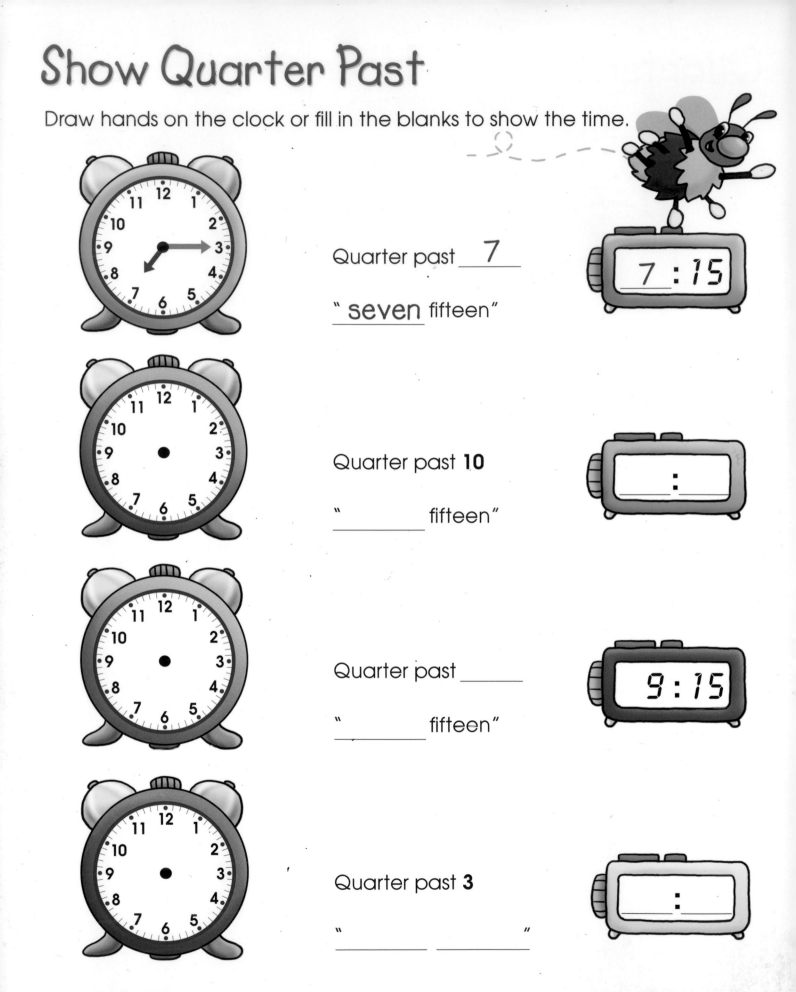

Quarter past ___7___

" __seven__ fifteen"

7 : 15

Quarter past **10**

"_____ fifteen"

Quarter past _____

"_____ fifteen"

9:15

Quarter past **3**

"_____ _____"

Quarter to the Hour

When the minute hand points to **9**, it is a **quarter to** the hour.
The hour hand is closer to the next hour.

The time is **quarter to 3.**
It is 15 minutes to 3.
We can say: **"a quarter to 3"**

OR

It is 45 minutes after 2.
It is **2:45**.
We can say: **"two forty-five"**

Read the hour hand first. Then read the minute hand.
Write the time.

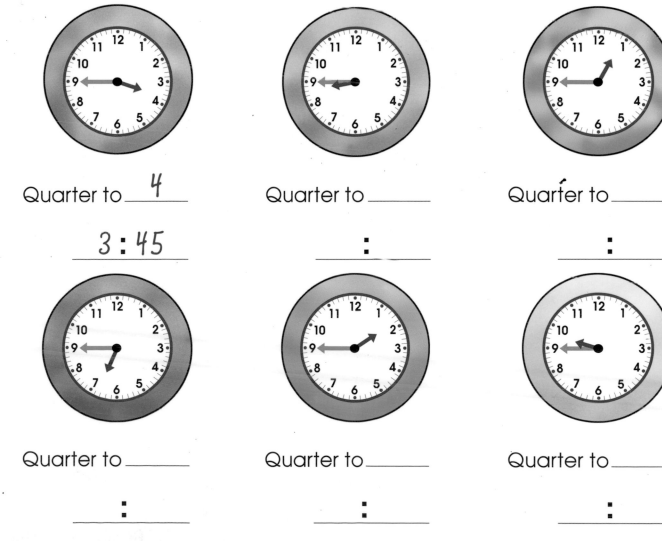

Quarter to __4__

3 : 45

Quarter to _____

___ : ___

Quarter to _____

___ : ___

Quarter to _____

___ : ___

Quarter to _____

___ : ___

Quarter to _____

___ : ___

Telling Quarter Hour Time

Write the time.

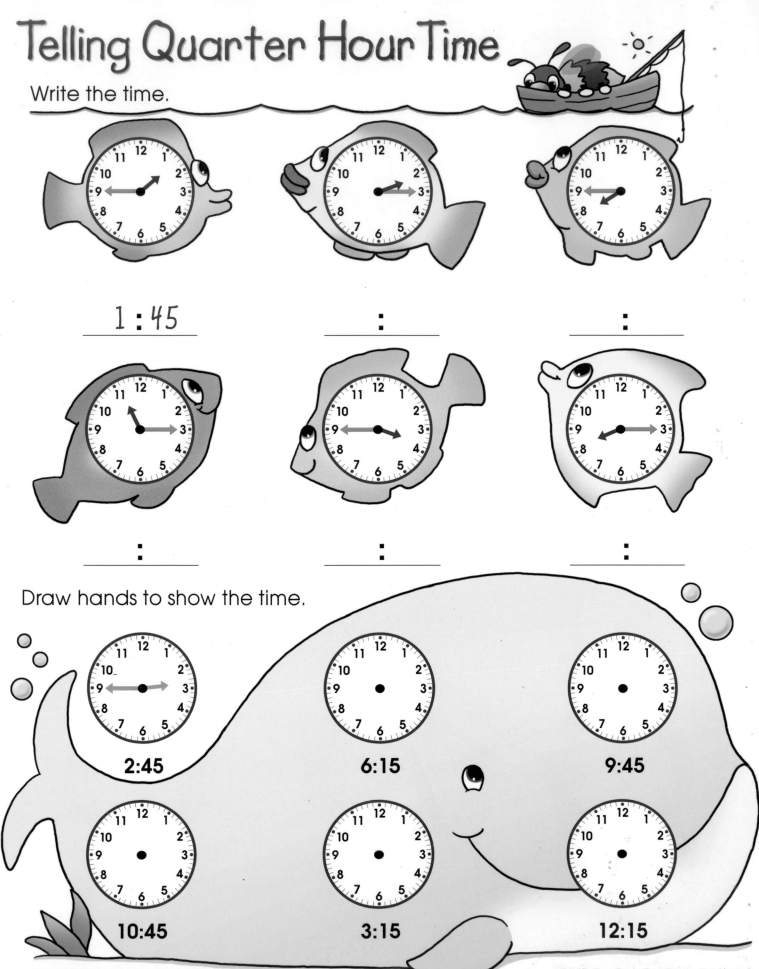

1 : 45   :   :

:   :   :

Draw hands to show the time.

2:45   6:15   9:45

10:45   3:15   12:15

Telling Time Quarter to the Hour

Time Goes By

Draw hands to show the end time and write the end time.

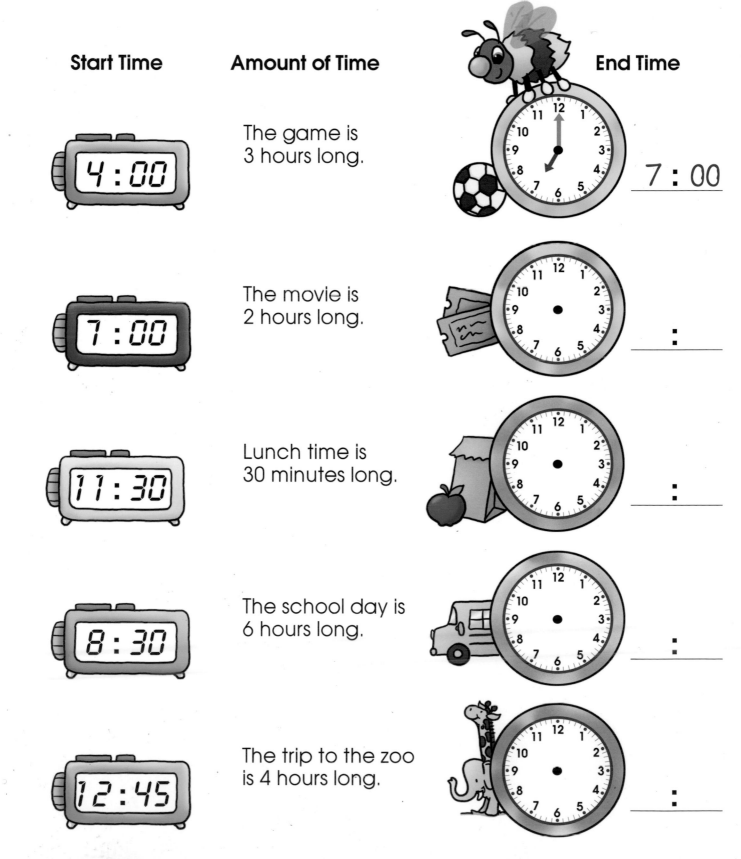

Start Time	Amount of Time		End Time
4:00	The game is 3 hours long.		7 : 00
7:00	The movie is 2 hours long.		:
11:30	Lunch time is 30 minutes long.		:
8:30	The school day is 6 hours long.		:
12:45	The trip to the zoo is 4 hours long.		:

Pennies, Nickels, and Dimes

Penny 1¢   1 cent

When we count **pennies**, we count by **ones**.

Nickel 5¢   5 cents

When we count **nickels**, we count by **fives**.

Dime 10¢   10 cents

When we count **dimes**, we count by **tens**.

Count the coins. Write the amount on the line.

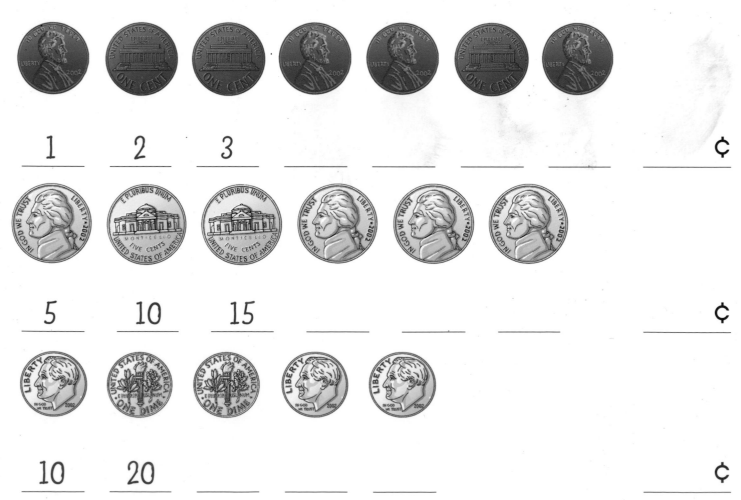

1   2   3   _____   _____   _____   _____ ¢

5   10   15   _____   _____   _____ ¢

10   20   _____   _____   _____ ¢

Counting Coins by Ones, Fives, and Tens

Can You Count These Coins?

What is the price of each toy?
Count the money. Write the total amount on the tag.

10   20   25   26   27   28

28¢

Counting 10¢, 5¢, and 1¢

Match the Amounts

Count the money in each purse.
Write the amount on the line.
Match the amount with the item.

Start with dimes, then count on with nickels and pennies.

33¢

36 ¢

53¢

GLUE

36¢

¢

61¢

¢

¢

30¢

46¢

¢

How Much is a Quarter?

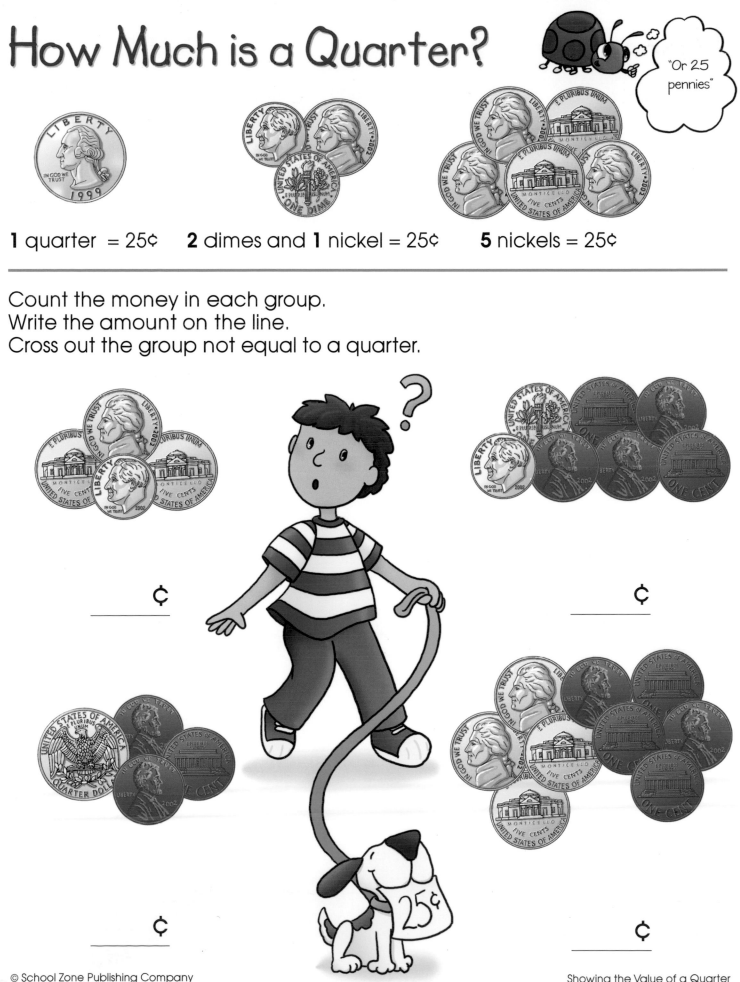

"Or 25 pennies"

1 quarter = 25¢   **2** dimes and **1** nickel = 25¢   **5** nickels = 25¢

Count the money in each group.
Write the amount on the line.
Cross out the group not equal to a quarter.

_____ ¢

_____ ¢

_____ ¢

_____ ¢

25¢

Showing the Value of a Quarter

More Quarters

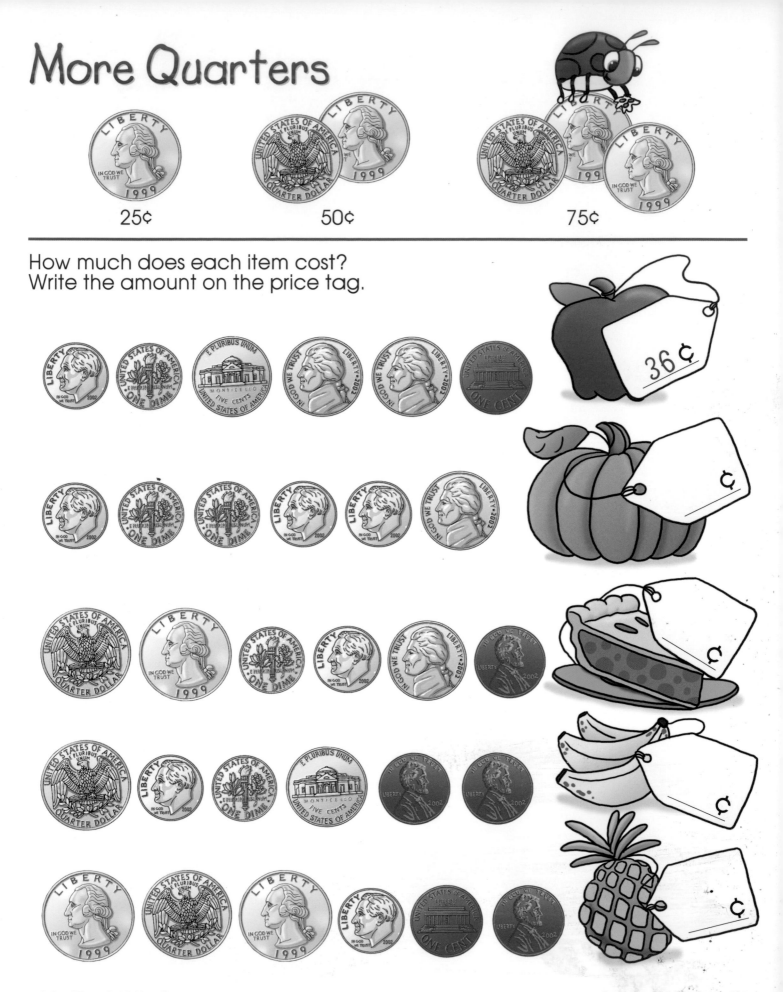

25¢

50¢

75¢

How much does each item cost?
Write the amount on the price tag.

36 ¢

___ ¢

___ ¢

___ ¢

___ ¢

Counting 25¢, 10¢, 5¢, and 1¢

Is There Enough?

Count the money. Is there enough money to pay for the item?

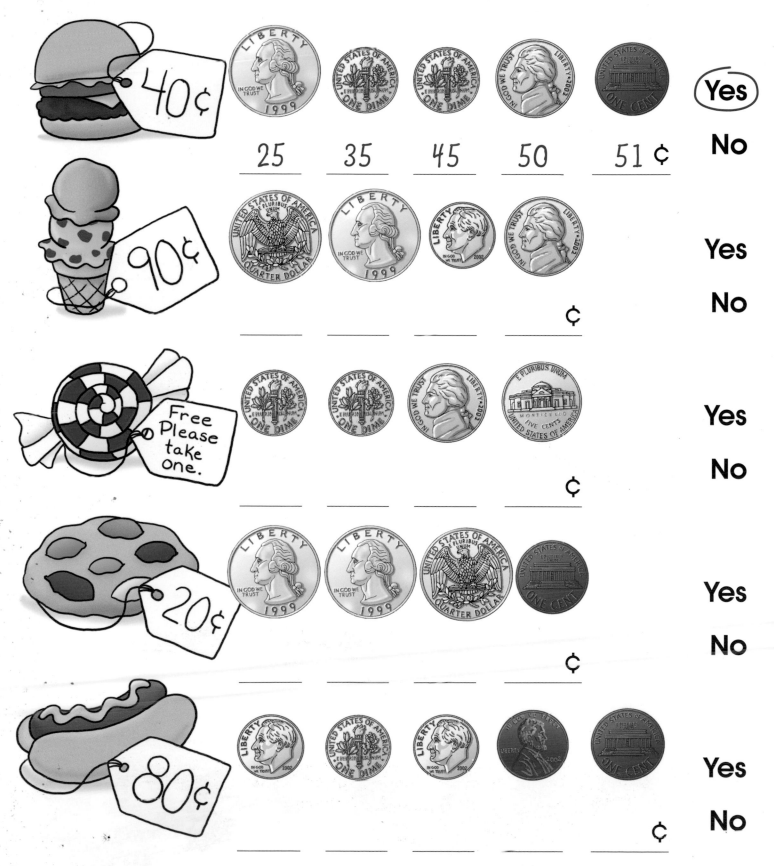

40¢ — 25 35 45 50 51 ¢ — **Yes** / No

90¢ — _____ ¢ — Yes / No

Free Please take one. — _____ ¢ — Yes / No

20¢ — _____ ¢ — Yes / No

80¢ — _____ ¢ — Yes / No

How Much is a Half Dollar?

"Or 50 pennies"

Half Dollar = 50¢   **2** quarters = 50¢   **5** dimes = 50¢   **10** nickels = 50¢

Circle the coins in each group to show 50¢.

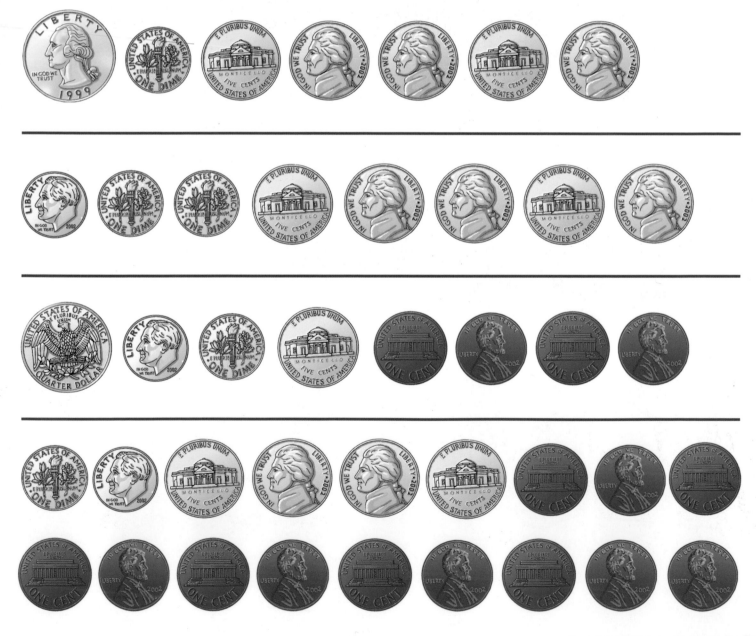

Showing the Value of a Half Dollar

Find Banks with 50¢

Count the money in each bank. Write the amount on the line.
Circle each amount that is equal to 50¢.

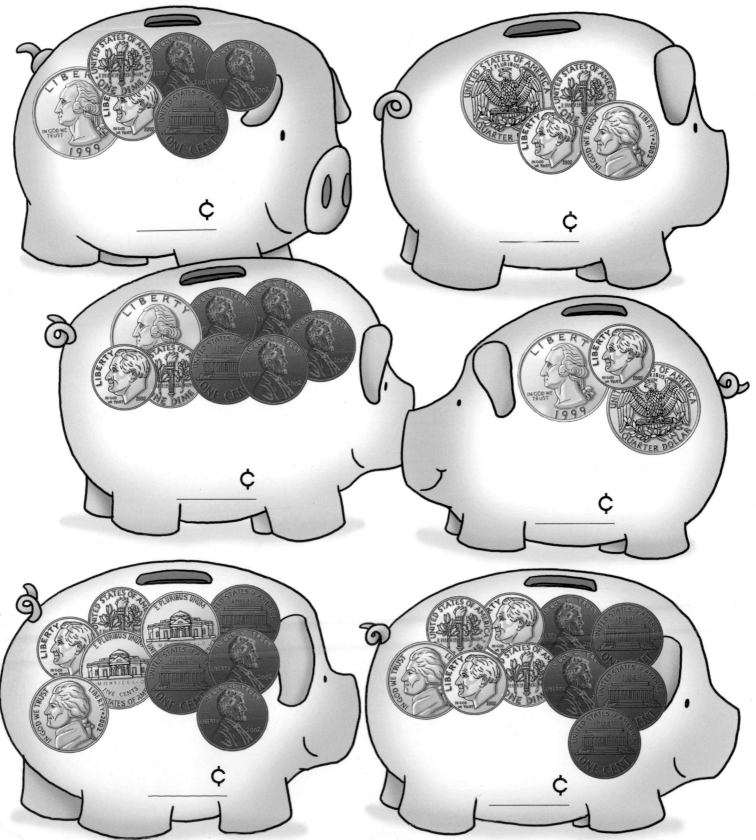

© School Zone Publishing Company

Finding Amounts Equal to 50¢

Which One Costs More?

Count the money. Write the amount on the line.
Circle the item that costs more.

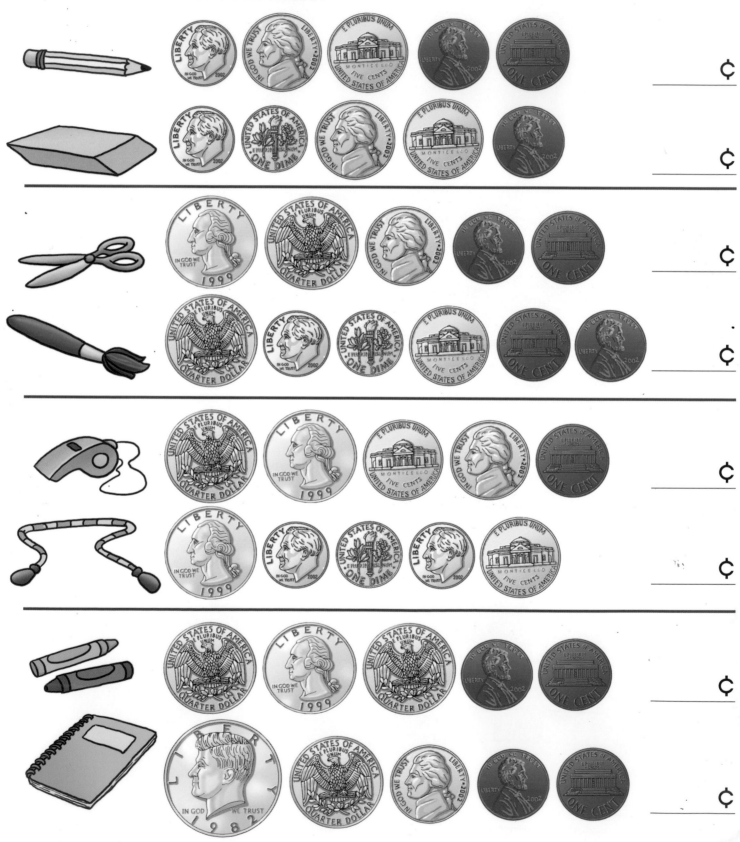

¢

¢

¢

¢

¢

¢

¢

¢

Counting Money; Comparing Amounts

Which Amount is Less?

Look at the two ways to show money.
Write the amount for each way.
Circle the amount that is less.

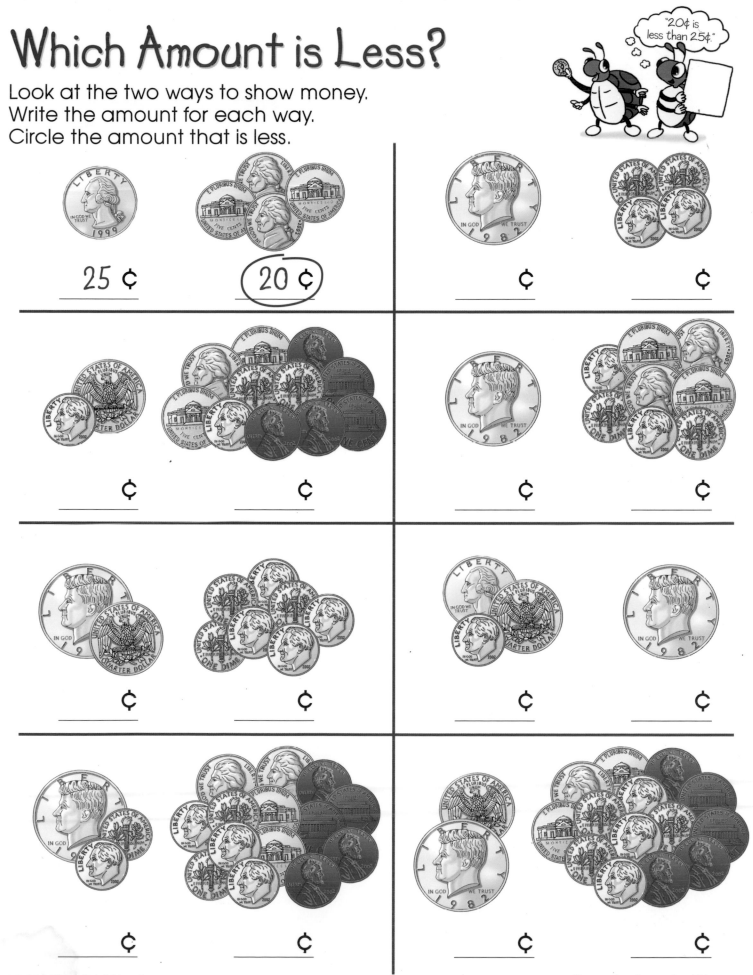

25 ¢   (20) ¢

____ ¢   ____ ¢

____ ¢   ____ ¢   ____ ¢   ____ ¢

____ ¢   ____ ¢   ____ ¢   ____ ¢

____ ¢   ____ ¢   ____ ¢   ____ ¢

Comparing Amounts of Money

What's Your Change?

Find the amount of change.
Write the amount.
Draw the coins.

Apples 20¢

Have	Buy	Change
	30¢	(N) 35 ¢ − 30 ¢ ____ 5 ¢
	37¢	¢ − ¢ ____ ¢
	35¢	¢ − ¢ ____ ¢
	69¢	¢ − ¢ ____ ¢
	79¢	¢ − ¢ ____ ¢

Finding Amount of Change